Life Around the World

What's School Like
Around the World?

By Kathleen Connors

New York

Published in 2022 by Cavendish Square Publishing, LLC
243 5th Avenue, Suite 136, New York, NY 10016

Copyright © 2022 by Cavendish Square Publishing, LLC

First Edition

No part of this publication may be reproduced, stored in a retrieval system, or transmitted in any form or by any means—electronic, mechanical, photocopying, recording, or otherwise—without the prior permission of the copyright owner. Request for permission should be addressed to Permissions, Cavendish Square Publishing, 243 5th Avenue, Suite 136, New York, NY 10016. Tel (877) 980-4450; fax (877) 980-4454.

Website: cavendishsq.com

This publication represents the opinions and views of the author based on his or her personal experience, knowledge, and research. The information in this book serves as a general guide only. The author and publisher have used their best efforts in preparing this book and disclaim liability rising directly or indirectly from the use and application of this book.

All websites were available and accurate when this book was sent to press.

Library of Congress Cataloging-in-Publication Data
Names: Connors, Kathleen, author.
Title: What's school like around the world? / Kathleen Connors.
Description: New York : Cavendish Square Publishing, [2022] | Series: Life around the world | Includes index.
Identifiers: LCCN 2020031841 | ISBN 9781502659323 (library binding) | ISBN 9781502659309 (paperback) | ISBN 9781502659316 (set) | ISBN 9781502659330 (ebook)
Subjects: LCSH: Schools–Juvenile literature.
Classification: LCC LB1556 .C66 2022 | DDC 371–dc23
LC record available at https://lccn.loc.gov/2020031841

Editor: Kristen Nelson
Designer: Tanya Dellaccio

The photographs in this book are used by permission and through the courtesy of: Cover Hugh Sitton/Stone/Getty Images; p. 5 Blend Images - JGI/Jamie Grill/Getty Images; p. 7 monkeybusinessimages/iStock/Getty Images Plus/Getty Images; p. 9 imtmphoto/iStock/Getty Images Plus/Getty Images; p. 11 Casarsa/iStock/Getty Images Plus/Getty Images; p. 13 Scott Peterson/Getty Images News/Getty Images; p. 15 The Packard Foundation /Handout/Getty Images Publicity/Getty Images; p. 17 ullstein bild/Getty Images; p. 19 YELIM LEE/AFP/Getty Images; p. 21 davidf/E+/Getty Images; p. 23 Catherine Delahaye/Stone/Getty Images.

Some of the images in this book illustrate individuals who are models. The depictions do not imply actual situations or events.

CPSIA compliance information: Batch #CS22CSQ: For further information contact Cavendish Square Publishing LLC, New York, New York, at 1-877-980-4450.

Printed in the United States of America

CONTENTS

Get Ready for School! 4

How Do They Get There? 10

School Days 14

Words to Know 24

Index 24

Get Ready for School!

It's the law for kids to go to school in the United States. That's the same in many places around the world. Still, there may be many differences between your school and one in another country!

Can you wear what you want to school? Almost all students in Great Britain wear a **uniform**. The uniform commonly shows the school's colors. Uniforms are worn in many other schools around the world too.

Most children in Japan and China also wear uniforms. In Japan, they may even carry the same school bag. Japanese students work hard during their classes in school. They also help to keep the school clean and make lunch!

How Do They Get There?

Children around the world get to school in different ways. In South Africa, some have to walk a long way. They may have to wait in a long line to take a **taxi**. This can make getting to school hard.

Students in Afghanistan often walk to school too. Then, their school day might only be a few hours long. That's partly because there aren't enough schools and teachers. Many children can't go to school at all.

School Days

Not all school days are the same. In India, it's common for students to start their day with a **prayer**. Then, the head of the school sometimes talks to the students. Music is often part of the day too.

In Finland, school days have a lot of time for playing. Teachers give students many short **recesses** during the school day. The children may go outside to play even in the winter!

In South Korea, many children take part in after-school study called *hagwon*. It helps them become even better at school subjects. It can mean a school day that goes into the nighttime!

Australian students have a summer break, just like in the United States. However, Australia's summer happens during America's winter! That's because Australia is in the Southern **Hemisphere**. Summer break is from December to late January.

A few things are the same at schools all over the world. Teachers and students work together so students learn the best they can. Students play together. Of course, most children have to do homework too!

WORDS TO KNOW

hemisphere: One-half of Earth.

prayer: Words spoken to a god or gods often to give thanks or praise.

recesses: Short periods of time during the school day in which children can play.

taxi: A car that takes people somewhere for money.

uniform: Special clothing worn by all members of a group.

INDEX

A
Afghanistan, 12

H
homework, 22

J
Japan, 8

S
South Africa, 10
South Korea, 18
summer break, 20

T
teachers, 12, 16, 22

U
uniform, 6, 8
United States, 4, 20

24

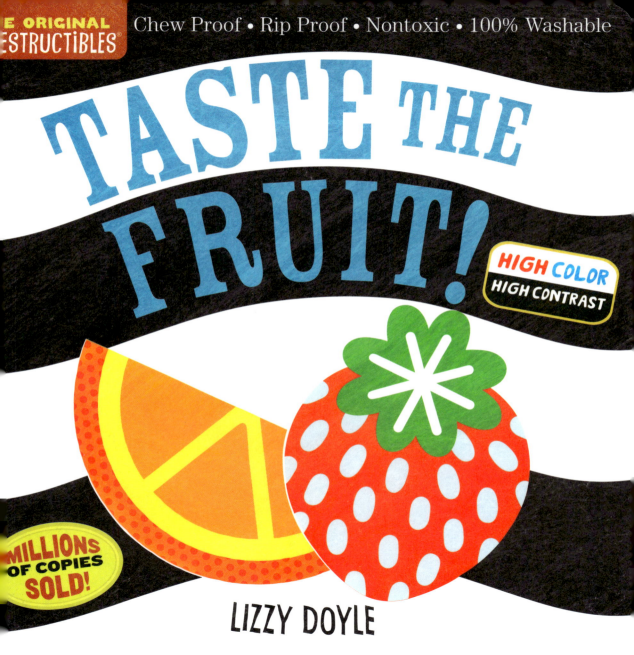

Red strawberries

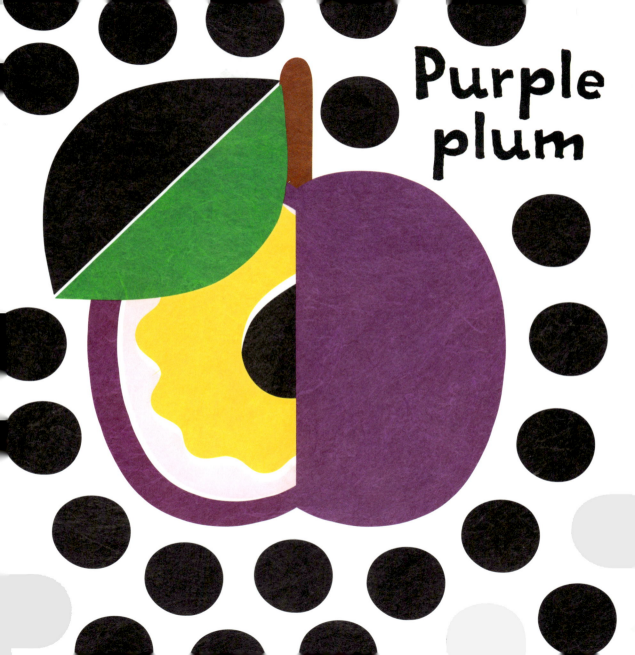

THE ORIGINAL INDESTRUCTIBLES®

For ages 0 and up!

Books babies can really sink their gums into!

Mmm, a *yellow* banana. So sweet!
Would you like a slice of *green* apple? So crisp!
Strawberries are bright *red*. So is a watermelon!
Learn all your favorite colors with a book that's INDESTRUCTIBLE.

DEAR PARENTS: High-Color, High Contrast INDESTRUCTIBLES nuture your baby's developing eyesight. And they're built for the way babies "read": with their hands and mouths. INDESTRUCTIBLES won't rip or tear and are 100% washable. They're made for baby to hold, grab, chew, pull, and bend.

CHEW ALL THESE AND MORE!

Copyright © 2022 by Indestructibles, LLC. Used under license. Illustrations copyright © 2022 by Workman Publishing Co., Inc.

All rights reserved. Library of Congress Cataloging-in-Publication Data is available. WORKMAN is a registered trademark of Workman Publishing Co., Inc., a subsidiary of Hachette Book Group, Inc.

Distributed in the United Kingdom by Hachette Book Group, UK, Carmelite House, 50 Victoria Embankment, London EC4Y 0DZ. Distributed in Europe by Hachette Livre, 58 rue Jean Bleuzen, 92 178 Vanves Cedex, France.

Contact special.markets@hbgusa.com regarding special discounts for bulk purchases.

All INDESTRUCTIBLES books have been safety-tested and meet or exceed ASTM-F963 and CPSIA guidelines. INDESTRUCTIBLES is a registered trademark of Indestructibles, LLC.

Cover © 2023 Hachette Book Group, Inc. First printing March 2022 | 10 9 8 7 6 5 4 3
Printed in China

$5.99 US / $8.99 Can.
ISBN 978-1-5235-1592-9

WORKMAN PUBLISHING CO., INC. 1290 Avenue of the Americas, New York, NY 10104 • indestructiblesinc.com